100 Things

you should know about

Inventions

100 Things

you should know about

Inventions

Duncan Brewer

Consultant: Barbara Taylor

MASON CREST PUBLISHERS INC.
370 Reed Road
Broomall, Pennsylvania 19008
(866)MCP-BOOK (toll free)
www.masoncrest.com

ISBN: 978-1-4222-1990-4
Series ISBN (5 titles): 978-1-4222-1992-8

First Printing
9 8 7 6 5 4 3 2 1

Cataloging-in-Publication Data on file with the Library of Congress.
Printed in the U.S.A.

First published as hardback in 2003 by Miles Kelly Publishing Ltd
Bardfield Centre, Great Bardfield, Essex, CM7 4SL

Editorial Director: Belinda Gallagher

Art Director: Jo Brewer

Assistant Editor: Lucy Dowling

Volume Designer: John Christopher, White Design

Artwork Commissioning: Bethany Walker

Copy Editor: Sarah Ridley

Proofreader: Hayley Kerr

Indexer: Jane Parker

Production Manager: Elizabeth Brunwin

Reprographics: Anthony Cambray, Stephan Davis,
Jennifer Hunt, Liberty Newton, Ian Paulyn

Editions Manager: Bethan Ellish

ACKNOWLEDGEMENTS
Cover artwork by Richard Burgess
All other images from the Miles Kelly Archives

Contents

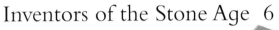

Inventors of the Stone Age

1 Humans have always been inventors. Over 400,000 years ago, our ancient relatives made stone tools such as axes. Then about 30,000 years ago, they discovered how to sew skins together to make clothes. Bones were first used as musical instruments over 20,000 years ago. Early people also learned how to use fire and invented cooking and ways of lighting the darkness. Because they lived by hunting animals, early humans invented bows and arrows to which they added sharp stone tips. They learned how to keep warm and dry by building shelters and homes made from tree branches, rocks and huge wooly mammoth tusks.

▶ Stone Age clothes were made out of animal skins sewn together using a bone needle.

The first tools

2 **The first inventors lived about 2.5 million years ago.** They were small, human-like creatures who walked upright on two legs. Their first inventions were stone tools. They hammered stones with other stones to shape them. These rough tools have been found in Tanzania in Africa. Scientists call this early relative of ours "handy man."

3 **Stone Age people made really sharp weapons and tools by chipping a stone called flint.** They dug pits and tunnels in chalky ground to find the valuable flint lumps. Their digging tools were made from reindeer antlers.

▶ Stone Age hunters trapped wooly mammoths in pits and killed them with spears.

4 **Early hunters were able to kill the largest animals.** With flint tips on their weapons, they overcame wild oxen and horses and even killed huge, wooly mammoths. They used their sharp flint tools to carve up the bodies. The flint easily sliced through tough animal hides.

◀ Flint tools were shaped to fit comfortably into the hand, with finely chipped cutting edges that could cut through large bones.

5 The axe was a powerful weapon. A new invention, the axe handle, made it possible to strike very hard blows. Fitted with a sharp stone head, the axe was useful for chopping down trees for firewood and building shelters.

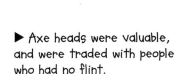

▶ Axe heads were valuable, and were traded with people who had no flint.

I DON'T BELIEVE IT!

Some Stone Age hunters used boomerangs! They made them out of mammoth tusks thousands of years before Australian boomerangs, and used them for hunting.

6 Saws could cut through the hardest wood. Flint workers discovered how to make very small flint flakes. They fixed the flakes like teeth in a straight handle of wood or bone. If the teeth broke, they could fix new ones. Saws were used to cut through tough bones as well as wood.

▼ Saws were made from about 12,000 BCE and had flint "teeth" held in place by resin.

The fire makers

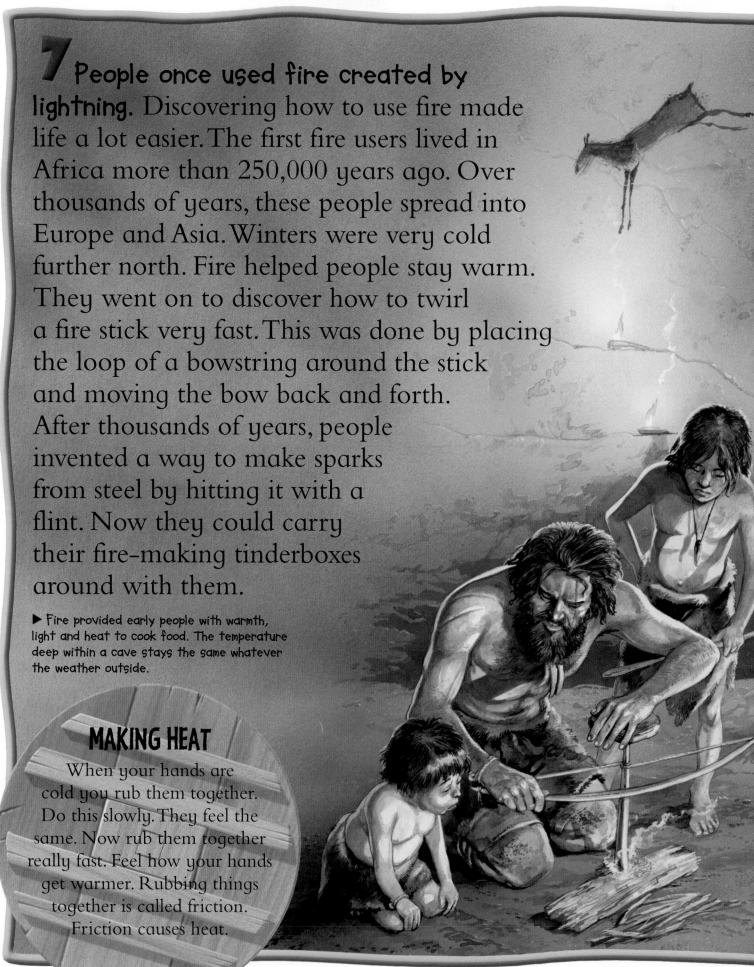

7 **People once used fire created by lightning.** Discovering how to use fire made life a lot easier. The first fire users lived in Africa more than 250,000 years ago. Over thousands of years, these people spread into Europe and Asia. Winters were very cold further north. Fire helped people stay warm. They went on to discover how to twirl a fire stick very fast. This was done by placing the loop of a bowstring around the stick and moving the bow back and forth. After thousands of years, people invented a way to make sparks from steel by hitting it with a flint. Now they could carry their fire-making tinderboxes around with them.

▶ Fire provided early people with warmth, light and heat to cook food. The temperature deep within a cave stays the same whatever the weather outside.

MAKING HEAT

When your hands are cold you rub them together. Do this slowly. They feel the same. Now rub them together really fast. Feel how your hands get warmer. Rubbing things together is called friction. Friction causes heat.

8 **Fire makes food taste good.**
The invention of cooking made food safer, because cooking kills germs. Cooking roots and meat on a fire makes them more tender as well as tastier. Humans are the only animals that cook food.

9 **Humans invented lamps to light deep, dark caves.** The lamps were saucers of clay or stone that burned animal fat, with moss for a wick. Campfire flames kept wild animals away at night. They also cooked food and kept people warm. People could see to make wall paintings in the caves.

New ways of moving

10 **With wheels, you can move enormous weights.** Once, heavy weights were dragged along the ground, sometimes on sleds. In Scandinavia, parts of 7,000-year-old sleds have been found. Over 5,500 years ago, the Sumerians of Mesopotamia began to use wheels made from carved planks fastened together.

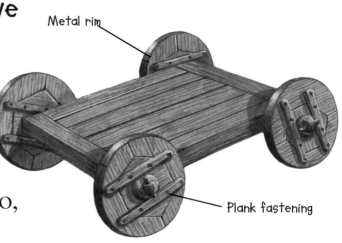

Metal rim

Plank fastening

▲ Plank wheels were very heavy, and metal rims helped hold them together.

▼ Spoked wheels made chariots light, fast and easy to steer.

11 **Warriors had light, strong wheels on their fighting chariots.** Wheels with spokes are lighter than solid plank wheels. From about 1800 BCE, the ancient Egyptians were using light chariots with spoked wheels. Horses pulled them fast in battle. The ancient Greeks and Romans used them for chariot races as well as for fighting.

Spoke   Light rim   Lightweight frame

Hobby (1818)

Velocipede (1861)
(Boneshaker)

Penny Farthing (early 1870s)

Mountain bike (1976)

◄ From the earliest boneshaker to today's mountain bike, the bicycle has always been popular.

12

Railway lines were once made of wood! Wheels move easily along rails. Horses pulled heavy wagons on these wagonways over 400 years ago. William Jessop invented specially shaped metal wheels to run along metal rails in 1789. Modern trains haul enormous loads at great speed along metal rails.

13

In 1861, bikes with solid tires were called boneshakers! However, an even earlier version of the bicycle was invented by the Frenchman, Count of Sivrac, in 1790. It had no pedals and was moved by the feet pushing against the ground. The invention of air-filled rubber tires made cycling more comfortable.

14

Cars with gigantic wheels can drive over other cars! Big wheels give a smooth ride. At some car shows, trucks with enormous wheels compete to drive over rows of cars. Tractors with huge wheels were invented to drive over very rough ground.

WHICH CAME FIRST?

1 (a) the chariot, or (b) the sled?

2 (a) solid wheels, or (b) spoked wheels?

3 (a) rails, or (b) steam engines?

4 (a) tires with inner-tubes, or (b) solid tires?

5 (a) the boneshaker, or (b) the mountain bike?

Answers:
1b 2a 3a 4b 5a

► Wheels this size are usually only found on giant dump trucks. These carry heavy loads such as rocks or soil that can be tipped out.

Harvesting the Earth

15 **The first farmers used digging sticks.** In the area now called Iraq, in about 9000 BCE, farmers broke the ground and planted seeds of wheat and barley. They used knives made of flint flakes fixed in a bone or wooden handle to cut the ripe grain stalks. The quern was an invention for grinding grain into flour between two stones.

▲ Curved knives made of bone or wood were used for harvesting grain.

I DON'T BELIEVE IT!

Some Stone Age people invented the first refrigerators! They buried spare food in pits dug in ground that was always frozen.

16 **Humans pulled the first plows.** They were invented in Egypt and surrounding countries as early as 4000 BCE. Plows broke the ground and turned over the soil faster and better than digging sticks. Later on, oxen and other animals pulled plows. The invention of metal plows made plowing much easier.

◄ Plowed furrows made it easier to sow, water and harvest crops.

17 **New inventions changed farming forever.** For thousands of years, farming hardly changed. Then, about 300 years ago, there were many new inventions. One of these was a seed-drill, invented by Englishman Jethro Tull. Pulled by a horse, it sowed seeds at regular spaces in neat rows. It was less wasteful than the old method of throwing grain onto the ground.

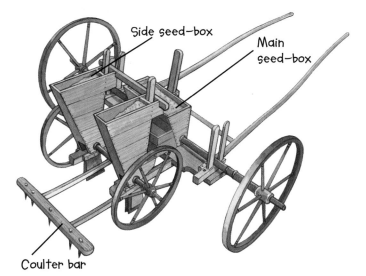

▲ Jethro Tull's seed-drill sowed three rows of seed at a time.

18 **Modern machines harvest huge fields of wheat in record time.** The combine harvester was invented to cut the crop and separate grain at the same time. Teams of combine harvesters roll across America's wide plains harvesting the wheat. What were once huge areas of land covered with grass now provide the grain for America's bread.

19 **Scientists are changing the way plants grow.** They have invented ways of creating crop plants with built-in protection from pests and diseases. Other bumper crop plants grow well in places where once they could not grow at all because of the soil or weather.

▼ The latest combine harvesters have air-conditioned, soundproofed cabs, and some even have sound systems.

Under attack!

20 Using an atlatl (a spear thrower) is like having an arm twice the normal length. Atlatls were invented in about 15,000 BCE. Hunters and warriors used them to hurl spears harder and farther than ever before. People all over the world invented this useful tool, and Australian Aborigines still use it.

◀ One end of the atlatl is cupped to hold the spear butt.

▼ Bowmen often stood behind lines of sharpened stakes that protected them from enemies on horseback.

21 Arrows from a longbow could pass through iron armor. Bows and arrows were invented at least 20,000 years ago. More than 900 years ago, the English longbow was made from a yew branch. Archers used it to fire many arrows a long distance in a short time. By law, all Englishmen had to practice regularly with the longbow. It helped them win many famous battles.

I DON'T BELIEVE IT!

Longbow archers could aim and fire six arrows per minute. The arrow sometimes went straight through an enemy's armor and out the other side.

22 Crossbows had to be wound up for each shot.

They were invented over 2,000 years ago in the Mediterranean area, and fired a metal bolt or short arrow. They were powerful and accurate, but much slower than longbows. Soldiers used them in sieges throughout Europe from about 1000 CE onward. But in battles, where speed was important, crossbows were often beaten by longbows.

▶ Crossbows were the first mechanical hand weapons, and at one time the Church tried to ban them.

23 In the Bible, David killed the giant, Goliath, with a pebble from a sling.

The sling is an ancient weapon probably invented by shepherds. They used it when guarding their flocks, and still do in some countries. The slinger holds the two loose ends and puts a pebble in the pouch. Then he whirls it around his head and lets go of one end. The pebble flies out at the target.

24 A schoolboy's catapult can do a lot of damage.

The rubber strips are like bowstrings, which can fire a pebble from a pouch, like a sling. Some anglers use a catapult to fire food to attract fish to the water's surface.

From stone to metal

25 Sometimes pieces of pure natural gold or copper can be found in the ground. The earliest metal workers, from about 8000 BCE, in the eastern Mediterranean, beat these metals with stone tools. They made the first copper weapons and gold ornaments.

▶ Gold is quite soft, and early goldsmiths beat it into a variety of shapes and made patterns of hammered indentations on its surface.

26 Blowing air onto flames makes them hotter. About 8,500 years ago, people discovered how to melt metals out of the rocks, or ores, containing them. They invented bellows—animal-skin bags, to blow air onto the flames. The hot flames melted the metal out of the ore. We call this "smelting" the metal.

27 Bronze weapons stay sharper for longer than copper ones. About 5,500 years ago, metal workers invented bronze by smelting copper ores and tin ores together. They used the bronze to make hard, sharp swords, spearheads and axe heads.

◀ Molten bronze was poured into molds of stone or clay to make tools.

▶ Bronze axes were sharper and less easily damaged than stone ones.

28 **Armies with iron weapons can beat armies with bronze weapons.** Iron is harder than bronze, but needs a very hot fire to smelt it. About 1500 BCE, metal workers began to use charcoal in their fires. This burns much hotter than ordinary wood and is good for smelting iron.

▲ After smelting, iron was beaten into shape to make strong, sharp weapons.

◀ Iron chains are made by hammering closed the red-hot links.

29 **The Romans were excellent plumbers.** They made water pipes out of lead instead of wood or pottery. Lead is soft, easily shaped and is not damaged by water.

30 **Some modern steelworks are the size of towns.** Steel is made from iron, and was first invented when small amounts of carbon were mixed into molten iron. Steel is very hard, and used to build many things, including ships and skyscrapers.

▶ Molten steel is poured from huge vats and rolled out into long sheets.

Boats and sails

31 **Viking explorers reached America 1,000 years ago.** The world's first boats were log rafts, useful for carrying heavy loads, but very slow. Viking boats were fast, and could travel far across the open sea. Sails were invented at least 5,000 years ago, and the Vikings used both sails and oars.

▶ Viking boats were made of long planks fitted onto wooden frames, and steered by means of a long oar fastened near the stern (back of the ship). They could be sailed across deep oceans, or rowed up shallow rivers, and made river journeys from the Baltic as far as the Black Sea.

I DON'T BELIEVE IT!

In 450 BCE, a merchant called Himilco sailed from North Africa to Britain. He ended up in Cornwall and bought Cornish tin!

32 About 300 years ago, sailing ships sailed all the world's oceans. Some, like the British man-of-war fighting ships, were enormous, with many sails and large crews of sailors. Countries such as Britain, France, Spain and Holland had large navies made up of these ships.

33 Some sailing boats race around the world non-stop. Modern sailing boats use many inventions, such as machines to roll up the sails and gears that allow the boat to steer itself. These boats are tough, light and very fast.

Wonderful clay

34 **Stone Age hunters used baked clay to do magic.** At least 30,000 years ago in Central Europe, they discovered that some clay went hard in the sun, and even harder in a fire. They made little clay figures of animals and humans. These were probably used in magic spells to help the hunters catch food. Hardening clay in a fire was the start of the invention of pottery.

◄ Some early clay figures may have been made to represent ancestors or gods and goddesses.

► Kilns produced much higher temperatures than open fires, and the heat could be controlled.

35 **Hard clay bowls changed the way people ate.** The first known pots were made around 10,000 BCE in Japan. They were shaped by hand and hardened in fires. They could hold liquid, and were used to boil meat and plants. This made the food tastier and more tender. Around 7000 BCE, potters in Southeast Asia used a new invention—a special oven to harden and waterproof clay, called a kiln.

36 **Potters' wheels were probably invented before cart wheels.** About 3500 BCE in Mesopotamia (modern Iraq), potters invented a wheel on which to turn lumps of clay and shape round pots. By spinning the clay, the potter could make smooth, perfectly round shapes quickly.

Clay pot

Heat duct

Fuel

37 Brick-making was invented in hot countries without many trees. The first brick buildings were built in 9000 BCE in the Jordan Valley. House builders made bricks from clay and straw, and dried them in the hot sun. By 3500 BCE, bricks hardened in kilns were used in important buildings in Mesopotamia.

▶ With the invention of bricks, it was possible to construct large buildings. In 6000 BCE, the Turkish town of Çatal Hüyük had houses with rooftop openings connected by ladders instead of doors.

Flat roof

Trap door

Ladder

Roof beams

38 Modern factories make thousands of pots at a time. They are "fired" in huge kilns. Wheels with electric motors are used, though much factory pottery is shaped in molds. Teams of workers paint patterns.

▼ Decorating pottery by hand and reproducing the pattern accurately requires much skill.

MAKE A COILED POT

Roll modelling clay into a long "snake" shape. Coil some of it into a flat circle. Continue to coil, building the coils upward. Try and make a bowl shape, and finally smooth out the ridges.

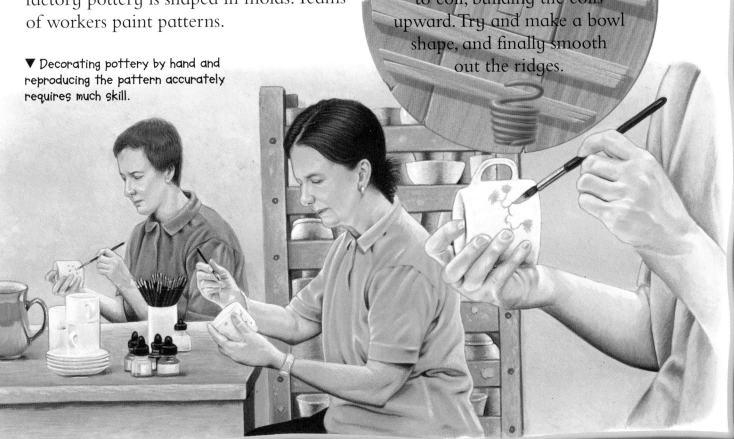

Sailing into the unknown

39 **Early sailors looked at the stars to find their way about.** Around 1000 BCE, Phoenician merchants from Syria were able to sail out of sight of land without getting lost. They knew in which direction certain stars lay. The north Pole Star, in the Little Bear constellation (star group), always appears in the north.

▲ Two stars in the Great Bear constellation are called the Pointers. They point to the north Pole Star in the Little Bear constellation.

40 **Magnetic compasses always point north and south.** They allow sailors to navigate (find their way) even when the stars are invisible. The Chinese invented the magnetic compass about 3,000 years ago. It was first used in Europe about 1,000 years ago.

▶ Using stick and shell maps, Pacific islanders successfully crossed thousands of kilometres of ocean.

▶ Compasses have a magnetized needle placed on a pivot so it can turn easily. Beneath this is a card with marked points to show direction.

41 **Early maps showed where sea monsters lived.** The first world map was drawn by the Greek Ptolemy in 160 CE. Greek maps from around 550 BCE showed the known world surrounded by water in which monsters lived. Over 500 years ago, Pacific islanders had maps of sticks and shells, showing islands and currents. The first globe was invented in 1492 by a German, Martin Behain.

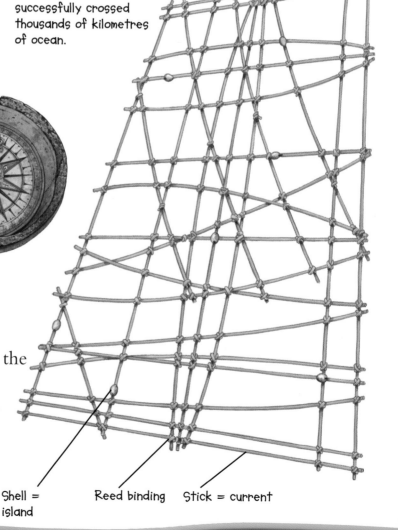

Shell = island

Reed binding

Stick = current

▼ The chronometer was invented by Englishman John Harrison in 1735. It was a reliable timepiece, specially mounted to remove the effect of a ship's motion at sea.

▶ The sextant was developed in the mid-1700s and was an important navigation aid until the 1900s.

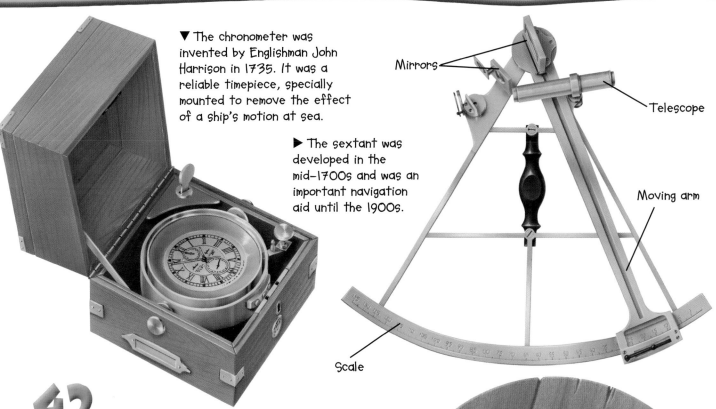

Mirrors

Telescope

Moving arm

Scale

42 **Eighteenth-century sailors could work out exactly where they were on the oceans.** They used an instrument called a sextant, invented in 1731. The sextant measured the height of the Sun from the horizon. The chronometer was an extremely reliable clock that wasn't affected by the motion of the sea.

43 **New direction-finding inventions can tell anyone exactly where they are.** A hand-held instrument, called a GPS receiver, receives signals from satellites in space. It shows your position within a few meters. These receivers can be built into cars, ships, planes—even laptop computers!

USING A COMPASS

Take a compass outside and find out which direction is north. Put a cardboard arrow with "N" on it on the ground pointing in the right direction. Then try to work out the directions of south, west and east.

Earth

Satellite orbit

Global Positioning Satellite (GPS)

◀ Modern navigation instruments use signals from several satellites to pinpoint their position.

Weapons of war

44 **The Romans invented massive rock-hurling weapons.** In medieval times, armies in Europe and the Middle East still used the same weapons in city and castle sieges. The trebuchet slung great rocks or burning material over city walls. The ballista fired missiles such as stones or spears with huge force at the enemy.

45 **The first gunpowder was used in fireworks.** The Chinese invented gunpowder over 1,000 years ago. In 1221, they used it to make exploding bombs, and in 1288, they invented the first gun, a cannon. Cannons and mortars, which fired bombs or large stone balls very high through the air, were used in European sieges from the 14th century onward. The first small firearms carried by soldiers appeared in the 15th century.

46 **The battering ram could smash through massive city walls and gates.** The Egyptians may have invented it in 2000 BCE to destroy brick walls. It was a huge tree-trunk, often with an iron head, swung back and forth in a frame. Sometimes it had a roof to protect the soldiers from rocks and arrows from above.

Siege tower

Ballista

▶ Medieval sieges of well-protected forts or cities sometimes lasted for months.

47 **Greek fire was a secret weapon that burned in water.** The Greeks invented it in the 7th century CE to destroy ships attacking Constantinople. A chemical mixture was squirted at enemies through copper pipes. It was still being used many centuries later in medieval sieges, pumped down onto the heads of attackers.

48 **Gunpowder was used in tunnels to blow up castle walls.** Attackers in a siege dug tunnels under the walls and supported them with wooden props. Then, they blew up or burned away the props so that the walls collapsed.

▶ The Gatling gun could fire six bullets a second.

49 **Modern machine guns can fire thousands of bullets per minute.** Richard Gatling, an American, invented the first machine gun in 1862. As in all modern guns, each machine-gun bullet has its own metal case packed with deadly explosives.

Trebuchet

Battering ram

Measuring time

50 **The huge stone slabs of Stonehenge can be used as a calendar.** Some of its stones are lined up with sunrise on the longest day of the year. It was built and rebuilt in Wiltshire in southern England between 3000 BCE and 1550 BCE.

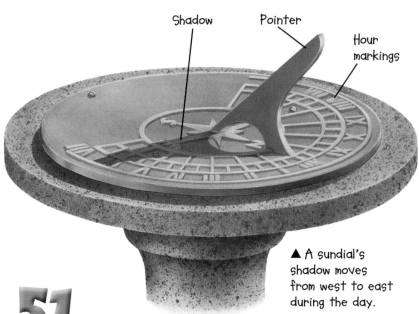

Shadow   Pointer   Hour markings

▲ A sundial's shadow moves from west to east during the day.

51 **One of the earliest clocks was a stick stuck in the ground.** Invented in Egypt up to 4,000 years ago, the length of the shadow showed the time of day. Later sundials had a face marked with hours, and a pointer that cast a shadow.

▼ Raising the huge main stones of Stonehenge required the muscles of many workers and the know-how of skilled Bronze Age engineers.

52

Candles, water and sand can all be used to tell the time. In 1400 BCE, the Egyptians invented a clock that dripped water at a fixed rate. Candle clocks were marked with rings, and in the hourglass, invented in about 1300 CE, sand ran between two glass globes.

▶ A candle clock (below) and an hourglass (right) show a time period has passed, not the time of day.

▼ Until the invention of quartz movements, wristwatches contained springs and cogs.

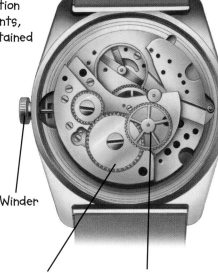

Winder

Main spring

Gear wheel

Ratchet wheel

53

You can't see any moving parts in a modern quartz clock. Early clocks depended on movement. A Dutchman, Christiaan Huygens, invented a clock in 1656 that depended on a swinging pendulum. About the same time, clocks driven by coiled springs were invented. Modern quartz crystal clocks work on invisible vibrations and are very accurate. They were first produced in 1929.

▶ Wrist watches were not made until 1790. Many modern watches have a liquid crystal display (LCD) and show changing numerals instead of hour and minute hands.

MAKE A SHADOW CLOCK

Fix about 2 feet (60 centimeters) of a garden stick upright in a flat piece of ground. Use lollipop sticks or twigs to mark the length of the shadow every hour, from 9 a.m. to 4 p.m. if possible. Which hour casts the shortest shadow?

Answer:
12 o'clock midday

54

Some clocks are like toys. Swiss cuckoo clocks contain a bird on a spring that flies out of a little door and "cuckoos" the time. Some 18th-century clocks looked like ships, and their guns fired to mark the hours.

Harvesting nature's energy

55 **The first inventions to use wind-power were sailing boats.** Invented around 3500 BCE by the Egyptians, and also by the Sumerians of Mesopotamia, the first sailing boats had a single square sail. By 600 CE, windmills for grinding grain had been invented in Arab countries. Some European windmills, in use from about 1100 CE onward, could be turned to face the wind.

56 **The first waterwheels invented were flat, not upright.** Used around 100 BCE in Yugoslavia and Albania, they needed very fast streams to drive them. One century later, Roman upright waterwheels worked better and had gears to slow them down. As well as grinding corn, some were used to drive pumps or saws.

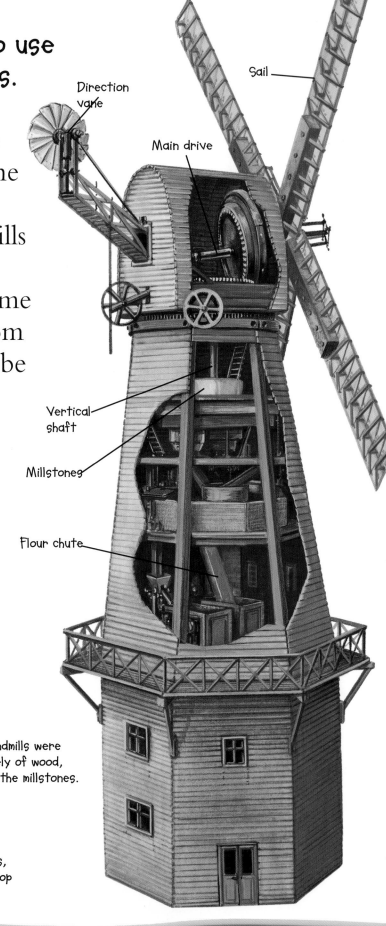

Direction vane

Sail

Main drive

Vertical shaft

Millstones

Flour chute

▶ Many windmills were made entirely of wood, apart from the millstones.

◀ In overshot watermills, the water strikes the top of the millwheel.

57 **Early steam engines often threatened to explode.** Thomas Savery's 1698 steam pump, invented in Devon, England, wasted fuel and was dangerous. Englishman Richard Trevithick developed a steam engine to move on tracks in 1804.

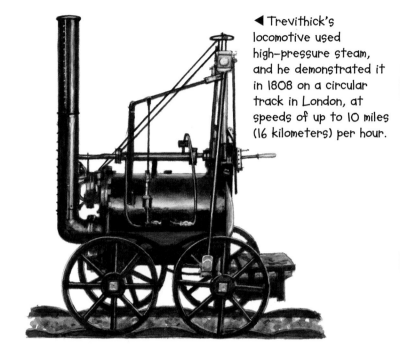

◄ Trevithick's locomotive used high-pressure steam, and he demonstrated it in 1808 on a circular track in London, at speeds of up to 10 miles (16 kilometers) per hour.

58 **Spinning magnets can create an electric current.** Michael Faraday and other scientists invented the first magnetic electricity generators (producers) in the 1830s. Today, huge dams use the power of millions of tons of flowing water to turn electricity generating machinery. They still use moving magnets to make electricity.

59 **The strength of the wind usually increases the higher up you are.** Some of the largest wind turbines in use today stand as high as a 20-story building, with propellers spanning more than the length of a football field. They produce enough electricity to power 1,400 homes or more.

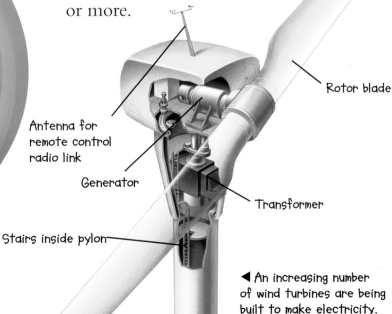

Rotor blade

Antenna for remote control radio link

Generator

Transformer

Stairs inside pylon

◄ An increasing number of wind turbines are being built to make electricity.

Marks on a page

▼ Phoenician

▼ Classical Greek

▼ Roman

ABCDEF

▼ Cyrillic

АБВГДЕ

▼ Modern Hebrew

▼ Modern Arabic

▼ Ancient Egyptian

▼ Chinese

人 月 子 水 雨 木

▼ Japanese

星 面 海 水 下

▲ Ancient picture writing used hundreds of different signs, but most modern alphabets have far fewer letters.

60 **The first writing was made up of pictures.** Writing was invented by the Sumerians 5,500 years ago. They scratched their writing onto clay tablets. The most famous word pictures are the "hieroglyphs" of ancient Egyptians from about 5,000 years ago. Cuneiform writing was made up of wedge shapes pressed into clay with a reed. It followed the Sumerian picture writing.

▲ Some of the religious books handwritten by monks were decorated with beautiful illustrations.

61 **The world's first book was a roll of paper made from reeds.** It was produced in Egypt between 1500 BCE and 1350 BCE and was called "The Book of the Dead." Christian monks used to write their religious books on sheets of parchment made from animal skins.

◄ The first printing presses were made of wood and used movable wooden letters.

62
Reading suddenly became much more popular after the invention of printing. A German, John Gutenberg, was an early inventor of a printing press with movable letters in the 15th century. By the end of the century, there were printing presses all over Europe.

63
Once, people were experts at doing sums on their fingers. The first written numbers were invented about 3100 BCE by Middle Eastern traders. Around 300 CE, the Chinese invented a counting machine called an abacus. It was a frame with beads strung on wires. Some people still use them.

I DON'T BELIEVE IT!

Some early Greek writing was called, "the way an ox plows the ground." It was written from right to left, then the next line went left to right, and so on, back and forth.

◄ Experts can do complicated sums very fast on an abacus.

64
Computers do sums at lightning speed. Early modern computers were invented in the United States and Europe in the 1930s and 1940s. Today, computers are small, cheap and extremely powerful. They can store whole libraries of information. The Internet allows everyone to share information and send email messages immediately almost anywhere in the world.

Making things bigger

65 **Small pieces of glass can make everything look bigger.** Eye-glass makers in Italy in the 14th century made their own glass lenses to look through. These helped people to read small writing. Scientists later used these lenses to invent microscopes, to see very small things, and telescopes, to see things far away.

▲ Eye glasses became important as more people began to read books.

66 **Scientists saw the tiny bacteria that cause illness for the first time with microscopes.** The Dutch invented the first microscopes, which had one lens. In the 1590s Zacharias Janssen of Holland invented the first microscope with two lenses, which was much more powerful.

67 **The Dutch tried to keep the first telescope a secret.** Hans Lippershey invented it in 1608, but news soon got out. Galileo, an Italian scientist, built one in 1609. He used it to get a close look at the moon and the planets.

▲ Early microscopes with two or more lenses, like those of English inventor Robert Hooke (1635-1703), were powerful, but the image was unclear.

QUIZ

1 Are lenses made from
(a) glass, or (b) steel?
2 Which came first,
(a) the telescope, or (b) eye glasses?
3 Do you study stars with
(a) a microscope, or (b) a telescope?
4 Which are smaller,
(a) bacteria, or (b) ants
5 Do modern microscopes make things look a) hundreds of times bigger, or b) thousands of times bigger?

Answers:
1a 2b 3b 4a 5b

68 You cannot look through a radio telescope. An American, Grote Reber, invented the first one and built it in his backyard in 1937. Radio telescopes pick up radio signals from space with a dish-shaped receiver. The signals come from distant stars, and, more recently, from space probes.

▲ Telescopes changed the mistaken idea that the Universe revolved around the Earth.

▼ An electron microscope can magnify a mosquito to monster size, and reveal tiny creatures that are normally invisible.

▲ Most radio telescope dishes can be moved to face in any direction.

69 Modern microscopes make things look thousands of times bigger. A German, Ernst Ruska, invented the first electron microscope in 1933. It made things look 12,000 times their actual size. The latest microscopes can magnify things millions of times.

Making music

70 **Humans are the only animals that play tunes on musical instruments.** Stone Age people invented rattles and other noise-makers, and made them from mammoth bones and tusks. Instruments you hit or rattle are called percussion instruments. They are still used in modern orchestras.

71 **Over 20,000 years ago Stone Age Europeans invented whistles and flutes.** They made them out of bones or antlers. Modern flutes still work in a similar way, by covering and uncovering holes in a tube while blowing down it.

72 **Some of the earliest harps invented were made from the shells of tortoises.** The first harps were played in Sumeria and Egypt about 5,000 years ago. Modern harps, like most ancient harps, have strings of different lengths.

Percussion

Trombone (brass section)

▼ The instruments of the modern orchestra are grouped in several sections and include the violin in the string section, the bassoon in the woodwind section and the trombone in the brass section.

Bassoon (woodwind section)

73 **Pianos have padded hammers inside, which strike the strings.** The first piano–like instrument was invented in about 1480 and its strings were plucked when the keys were pressed, not struck. It made a softer sound than a modern piano.

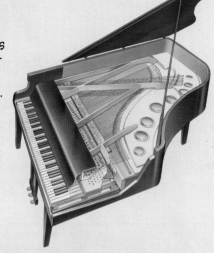

▶ The grand piano's strings are laid out horizontally in a harp–shaped frame.

74 **The trumpet is one of the loudest instruments in the orchestra.** A trumpet was found in Tutankhamen's tomb in Egypt dating back to 1320 BCE. Over 2,000 years ago, Celtic warriors in Northern Europe blew great bronze trumpets shaped like mammoth tusks to frighten their enemies.

75 **Bagpipes sound as strange as they look.** They were invented in India over 2,000 years ago. The Roman army had bagpipe players. In the Middle Ages, European and Middle Eastern herdsmen sometimes played bagpipes while they looked after their animals.

Violin (string section)

Conductor

Keeping in touch

76 Some African tribes used to use "talking drums" to send messages. Native Americans used smoke signals, visible several miles away. Before electrical inventions such as the telephone, sending long-distance messages had to be a simple process.

◀ Smoke from burning vegetation could be broken up into signals by lowering and raising a blanket over the smoke.

▶ Each position of the semaphore signaler's arms forms a different letter. What does this message say?

77 Wooden arms on tall poles across the country sent signals hundreds of miles in 18th-century France. Claude Chappe invented this system, now called semaphore, in 1797. Until recently, navies used semaphore flags to signal from ship to ship. In 1838, American Samuel Morse invented a code of short and long bursts of electric current or light, called dots and dashes. It could send messages along a wire, or could be flashed with a light.

78 The telephone can send your voice around the world. A Scotsman, Alexander Graham Bell, invented it in the 1870s. When you speak, your voice is changed into electric signals that are sent along to a receiver held by the other user. Within 15 years, there were 140,000 telephone owners in the United States.

1 = S
2 = I
3 = G
4 = N
5 = A
6 = L

79 Radio signals fly through the air without wires. An Italian, Guglielmo Marconi, invented the radio, or "wireless," in 1899. Radio stations send signals, carried on invisible radio waves, which are received by an antenna. A Scot, John Logie Baird, invented an early TV system in 1926. TV pictures can travel through the air or along wires.

Satellite

TV studio

NTBC

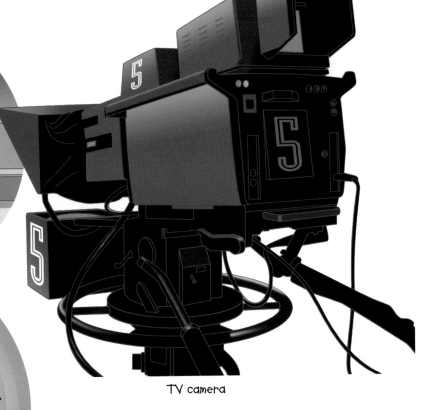

TV camera

I DON'T BELIEVE IT!

Early TV performers had to wear thick, clownlike makeup. The pictures were so fuzzy that viewers could not make out their faces otherwise.

▲ Live TV images can be beamed to a satellite in space, then redirected to the other side of the world.

80 With a cell phone, you can talk to practically anyone wherever you are. Your voice is carried on radio waves called microwaves and passed from antenna to antenna until it reaches the phone you are calling. Some of the antennas are on space satellites.

Taking to the skies

81 **The first hot−air balloon passengers were a sheep, a duck and a cockerel.** The French Montgolfier brothers invented the hot-air balloon in 1782. The first human passengers often had to put out fires, as the balloon was inflated by hot air created by burning straw and wool!

▲ The Montgolfier hot−air balloon made the first untethered, manned flight from Paris in 1783.

82 **Many inventors have tried to fly by flapping birdlike wings.** All have failed. One of the first bird-men crashed to his death at a Roman festival in the 1st century CE.

83 **The first aircraft flight lasted just 12 seconds.** The Wright brothers invented their airplane and flew it in 1903 in the United States. In 1909, a Frenchman, Louis Blériot, flew across the English Channel. In World War I, airplanes were used in combat. In World War II, aircraft such as the British Spitfire beat off German air attacks.

▲ Formed in 1965, the Royal Air Force Aerobatic Team, known as the Red Arrows, uses Hawk jets. They need perfect timing to perform their close formation flying and aerobatics at high speed.

84

The first model helicopter was made by Leonardo da Vinci as long ago as 1480. In 1877, an Italian, Enrico Forlanini, invented a steam helicopter which flew for 60 seconds and reached a height of 50 feet (15 meters). Modern helicopters can hover and land almost anywhere and are often used for rescue missions at land and sea.

85

In 1948, a jet plane flew faster than the speed of sound. Englishman Frank Whittle invented the first jet engine in 1930. Most modern aircraft are jets without propellers. Teams of jets, like the Red Arrows, often perform stunts at air shows.

I DON'T BELIEVE IT!

In 1783, the first hydrogen balloon was attacked and destroyed by terrified farm workers when it landed. It had flown 15 miles (24 kilometers).

Keeping a record

86 **The first sound recording was the nursery rhyme, "Mary had a little lamb."** In 1877, an American, Thomas Edison, invented a way of recording sounds by causing a needle to scratch marks on a cylinder or tube. Moving the needle over the marks again repeated the sounds. Performers spoke or sang into a horn, and the sounds were also played back through it.

▲ Thomas Edison produced many important inventions, including sound recording, electric light bulbs and an early film–viewing machine.

87 **To play the first disc records, you had to keep turning a handle.** Emile Berlin, a German, invented disc recording in 1887. The discs were played with steel needles, and soon wore out. They also broke easily if you dropped them. Long-playing discs appeared in 1948. They had 20 minutes of sound on each side and were made of bendy plastic, which didn't break so easily.

▼ Early record players had to be wound up between records, and the loudspeaker was a large horn.

QUIZ
1 Were the first recordings on (a) discs, or (b) cylinders?
2 Which came first, (a) movies, or (b) long-playing records?
3 Was the first photograph of (a) flowers, or (b) rooftops?
4 CDs are played with diamond needles —true or false?
5 Were the first movies shown in (a) the 19th century, or (b) the 20th century?

Answers:
1b 2a 3b 4 false 5a

88 It took eight hours to take the world's first photograph in 1826. Frenchman Joseph Nicéphore Niépce was the inventor, and the first photograph was of rooftops. Early cameras were huge, and the photos were on glass plates. In 1889, American George Eastman invented rolls of film, making photography much easier.

▲ Modern digital cameras have a display that shows the view the lens sees, which is the image that will be stored.

89 The forerunner of the iPod/MP3 player was the portable laser-based CD player. It was more than ten times bigger and heavier than an iPod. Moving it often made the compact disc (CD) skip.

▲ The Lumière brothers, who invented the movie projector, also made films and opened the first public cinema.

▶ Launched in 2001, the iPod took little more than one year to develop.

90 Only one person at a time could watch the first movies. The viewer peered through a hole in a box. Thomas Edison's company invented movies in 1888. The invention of a projector in 1895 by the French Lumière brothers allowed a whole audience to watch the film on a screen.

Round the house

91 **A horse and cart were needed to move the first successful vacuum cleaner around.** An English engineer, Hubert Cecil Booth, invented it in 1902. The first "Hoover" electric vacuum cleaner was built from a wooden box, an electric fan and an old sack in 1907 in America.

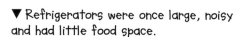
▼ Refrigerators were once large, noisy and had little food space.

▲ The first vacuum cleaners worked by opening and closing a bellows with a handle.

92 Early refrigerators, invented in the 19th century, killed many people. They leaked the poisonous gas that was used to cool them. In 1929, the gas was changed to a non-poisonous one called freon. We now know that freon causes damage to the planet's atmosphere, so that is being changed too.

QUIZ
1 Did the first "Hoover" need (a) a horse, or (b) an electric fan?
2 Were early refrigerators dangerous because (a) they blew up or (b) they leaked poison gas?
3 The Cretans had china toilets 4,000 years ago—true or false?
4 Do light bulbs contain (a) water (b) air, or (c) neither?
5 Who opened the first electric light company, (a) Thomas Twyford, or (b) Thomas Edison?

Answers:
1b 2b 3 false 4c 5b

93 A melted chocolate bar led to the invention of the microwave oven. An American, Percy L. Spencer, invented it in 1953 after noticing that a microwave machine where he worked had melted the chocolate in his pocket. In a microwave oven, the microwaves make the food heat itself up from the inside. Eggs may explode because of this.

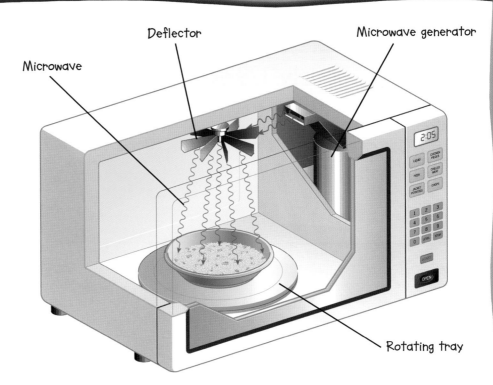

▲ In a microwave oven, the microwaves are deflected by metal vanes down onto the food below.

94 There is no air inside a light bulb. If there was, it would burn out in no time. The first light bulbs failed because air could get in. American Thomas Edison invented an air-tight light bulb in 1879 that could burn for a long time. He opened the first electric light company in 1882.

◄ In a light bulb, electricity causes a wire filament to glow brightly in the airless bulb.

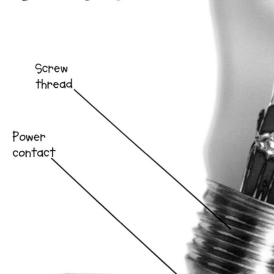

95 Four thousand years ago in Crete in Greece, the king's palaces had flushing toilets. They used rainwater. In England, toilets that flushed when you pulled a handle were invented in the 18th century. In 1885, Thomas Twyford invented the first all-china flushing toilet.

From Earth into space

96 Concorde was able to fly at twice the speed of sound, nearly 1,340 miles (2,150 kilometers) per hour. This is at least twice as fast as the earliest jets. The jet airliner crossed the Atlantic at a height of over 59,000 feet (18,000 meters).

◄ Concorde carried passengers in luxury across the Atlantic in a fraction of the usual air crossing time—under 3 hours. The plane is now retired.

97 Rockets helped the Chinese drive away a Mongol army in the 13th century. The rockets used gunpowder, which the Chinese had invented 300 years earlier but had only used in fireworks.

I DON'T BELIEVE IT!

A 15th-century Chinese man, Wan Hu, tried to make a flying machine out of 47 rockets and two kites. His servants lit all the rockets at the same time, and Wan Hu disappeared forever in a massive explosion.

◄ The Chinese were the first to use gunpowder in war, as in this hand-held gun for firing missiles.

98 German war rockets in World War II could travel 200 miles (321 kilometers) to hit England. They were invented by a scientist called Werner von Braun. After the war, he helped the United States build space rockets.

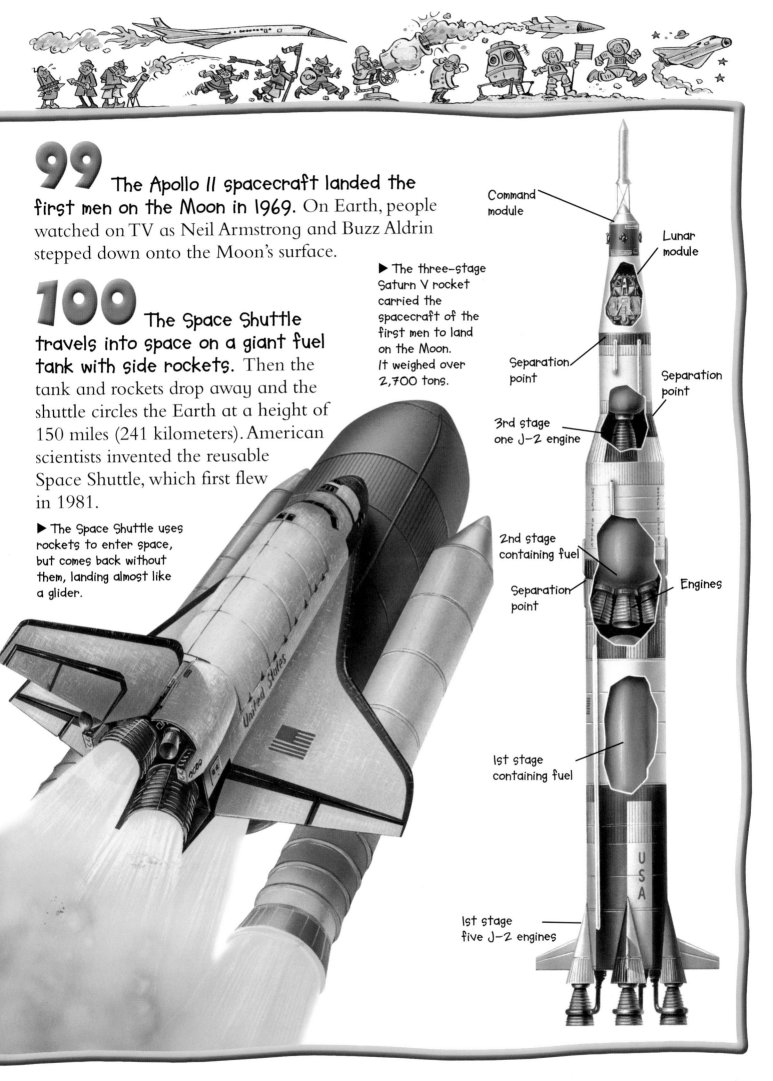

99
The Apollo II spacecraft landed the first men on the Moon in 1969. On Earth, people watched on TV as Neil Armstrong and Buzz Aldrin stepped down onto the Moon's surface.

100
The Space Shuttle travels into space on a giant fuel tank with side rockets. Then the tank and rockets drop away and the shuttle circles the Earth at a height of 150 miles (241 kilometers). American scientists invented the reusable Space Shuttle, which first flew in 1981.

▶ The Space Shuttle uses rockets to enter space, but comes back without them, landing almost like a glider.

▶ The three-stage Saturn V rocket carried the spacecraft of the first men to land on the Moon. It weighed over 2,700 tons.

Command module

Lunar module

Separation point

Separation point

3rd stage one J-2 engine

2nd stage containing fuel

Separation point

Engines

1st stage containing fuel

1st stage five J-2 engines

Index